Teaching With Favorite Franklin Books

BY KATHLEEN M. HOLLENBECK

D1518742

SCHOLASTIC
PROFESSIONAL BOOKS

NEW YORK • TORONTO • LONDON • AUCKLAND • SYDNEY
MEXICO CITY • NEW DELHI • HONG KONG • BUENOS AIRES

*f*or Eileen,

who made growing up

so much fun.

Front cover and interior design by Kathy Massaro
Interior illustrations by Maxie Chambliss

Contents

❧ INTRODUCTION ❧

Step into the world of Franklin, a lovable turtle who sees life through the eyes of a child. This resource book explores 12 titles from the popular Franklin series—stories that cover topics of real interest and real-life situations for children, such as starting school, making new friends, handling emotions, and telling the truth. As Franklin learns to ride a bike, children will learn about setting their own goals. When Franklin wants a pet, they'll explore possibilities and weigh aspects of pet care. With discussion and hands-on activities, children can explore and extend each story and theme—and strengthen skills in math, language arts, science, social studies, critical thinking, drama, and art in the process.

Meet the Author

Paulette Bourgeois

Born: July 20, 1951
Winnepeg, Canada

When asked what she hopes children will learn from her books, Paulette Bourgeois explains: "It is most important to look for the wonder in ordinary things." Some of this wonder, and a curious anxiety, spill over into her character Franklin. The world's best-loved turtle overcomes the challenges of the everyday life of a five-year-old in a way that resonates with children. Since 1986, Franklin and Paulette have championed a fear of the dark, boastful fibs, thunderstorms, new friends, museum dinosaurs...

When Paulette finished writing her first book, *Franklin in the Dark*, she knew that she would always write stories for children. With each new book, she imagines a child turning the last page and giving a satisfied sigh. Paulette explains: "I want readers to feel connected to my storybook world—to feel, to smell, to touch and to explore the landscapes, both internal and external, that I have created. As I write, I draw on my own experiences and find it easy to remember emotions and situations."

Although Paulette is best-known for the Franklin books, she is also a writer of fiction and nonfiction for young readers. In her nonfiction writing, she explores another realm of wonders with her young readers. She shares "amazing" information on many topics: from apples to potatoes; from fire fighters to garbage collectors; from the moon to the sun! What's next? The universe! *The Sun: Starting With Space* was shortlisted for a Science in Society Book Award (1995), given by the Canadian Science Writer's Association, and won the honor of Parents' Choice Approval (1997), given by the U.S. Parents' Choice Foundation. Currently, Paulette is endeavoring to write longer books for children, and trying to follow the advice she gives to children: "Read, read, read and write, write, write."

Profile of Paulette Bourgeois © 2001–1996 Scholastic Inc. All rights reserved.
Photo courtesy Pierre Gaudreau/Kids Can Press, Ltd.

About This Book

Each of the lessons in this book focuses on one of 12 books in the Franklin series. Here's what you'll find in each lesson:

◎ **Summary:** a brief synopsis of the featured Franklin book

◎ **The Story's Message:** suggested learning themes for the lesson

◎ **Before You Read:** suggestions for discussion and/or activities to prepare children for the story's theme

◎ **After You Read:** discussion tips and suggestions for helping children understand the story, focus on the theme, and relate both to their own lives

◎ **Activities:** a list of suggested activities for developing the theme and strengthening skills in math, science, language arts, social studies, critical thinking, drama, and art. A few activities require advance planning. Most can be done on the spot.

◎ **Book Links:** a list of picture books relating to the theme

Correlations to the Language Arts Standards

The activities in this book are designed to support you in meeting the following standards outlined by the Mid-Continent Regional Educational Laboratory (MCREL), an organization that collects and synthesizes national and state K–12 curriculum standards.

Uses the general skills and strategies of the reading process:

● Understands how print is organized and read
● Creates mental images from pictures and print
● Uses meaning clues to aid comprehension and make predictions about content

Uses reading skills and strategies to understand and interpret a variety of literary texts:

● Uses reading skills and strategies to understand a variety of familiar literary passages and texts, including fiction
● Knows main ideas or theme, setting, main characters, main events, sequence, and problems in stories
● Makes simple inferences regarding the order of events and possible outcomes
● Relates stories to personal experiences

Uses the general skills and strategies of the writing process:

● Uses writing and other methods to describe familiar persons, places, objects, or experiences
● Writes in a variety of forms or genres, including responses to literature

Source: *A Compendium of Standards and Benchmarks for K–12 Education* (Mid-Continent Regional Educational Laboratory, 1995)

Teaching Activities for Any Time

Use these activities with any of the lessons to reinforce additional skills across the curriculum.

Language Arts

Make Character Scrapbooks

Before the first lesson, staple 15 pieces of white paper together to form a character scrapbook for each child. Explain that the book will help children get to know characters in the Franklin books. Starting with the very first lesson, have children create a page for each character they meet. As children read the Franklin books, encourage them to add details to each character's scrapbook page, such as what the character likes to collect, favorite hobbies or interests, favorite books, favorite places to visit, people he or she admires, friends, awards or accomplishments, family members, and so on. Remind children to add new characters as they meet them.

Pocket Chart Phonics

Use pocket charts to reinforce phonics connections throughout. Focusing on one phonics topic at a time, find rhyming patterns, word families, digraphs, blends, synonyms, and more in the Franklin stories. Write the words children find on sentence strips and place them in the pocket chart. Depending on the topic, have children come up with additional words that rhyme, are part of word families, or represent digraphs or blends. You might also have children replace synonyms with words of the same meaning and substitute pictures for words to make a rebus.

Cumulative Skills

Franklin could count by twos and tie his shoes. What else could he do? On chart paper, have children help you list all the things Franklin could do from the first book onward. As you go through the books, keep a running list of the skills Franklin could do, as described in the opening paragraph of each story. (*slide down a riverbank, count forward and backward, zip zippers, button buttons, count by twos, tie his shoes, etc.*) By the last story, children will have a long list of Franklin's abilities. Which ones can they do as well?

Bring the Stories to Life

Provide drawing paper, crayons or markers, and plenty of time for imaginations to blossom! Have children design book jackets and comic strips to summarize or extend individual Franklin stories.

Science

Turtle Talk

Help children compare characteristics about Franklin that are real for turtles rather than "pretend." For example, Franklin eats fly pie and pancakes with flies. What's real: Turtles do eat flies. What's make-believe: the pancakes and pie. Cut a 6-inch circle out of cardboard or tagboard. Give one to each child. Have children write real facts about turtles on one side of the circle. On the flip side, have them write things Franklin does or enjoys that are make-believe. Add arms and legs to make the circle a turtle. Make a hole in each and hang the turtles from the ceiling with yarn.

Compare Animals

Divide the class into small groups. Ask each group to choose two animals from the Franklin books and compare/contrast them as they are in Franklin's world or in real life. Animals they might compare include: turtle, bear, moose, fox, beaver, rabbit, duck, goose, and skunk.

Animal Adventures

Brainstorm a list of other adventures Franklin or his friends might have, based on their animal characteristics or natural tendencies. Choose one adventure and write about it as a class or in small groups.

Math

Counting With Turtles

Your students will enjoy making and using these adorable turtle manipulatives for math. Over time, collect a large number of walnut shell halves. Provide students with craft glue, felt scraps, scissors, permanent markers, and other decorative materials. Invite children to add a head, eyes, feet, and tail to each shell. When it's time for math, take out the turtles!

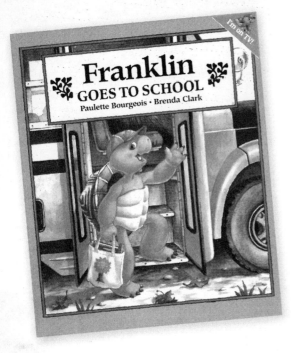

Franklin Goes to School

❧❧❧

(KIDS CAN PRESS, 1995)

Franklin feels anxious when he starts school for the very first time. As he meets his new teacher and explores the classroom, Franklin realizes that school is a wonderful place to learn.

The Story's Message

▲▲▲▲▲

◈ Believe in yourself and in what you can do.

◈ It can be fun to try something new.

Before You Read

Hold up *Franklin Goes to School* so children can see the cover. Ask: Who do you see in this picture? Some children may recognize Franklin. If not, explain that the story is going to be about a turtle named Franklin. Then let children find clues in the picture (such as the color of the school bus and the items in Franklin's book bag) to help them answer these questions: Where is Franklin going? What do you think this story is going to be about? Why do you think that?

After You Read

Ask questions to bring out the main points in the story— for example:

◎ How did Franklin feel before he left his house in the morning? What details in the story show you he felt this way?

◎ Why did Franklin suddenly feel afraid instead of excited about school? How could you tell that his feelings had changed?

◎ How did Mr. Owl help Franklin feel comfortable about being in school?

◎ Will Franklin be nervous to go to school tomorrow? Why do you think that?

◎ How did you feel the day you came to school for the very first time?

◎ What did you like most about school on that very first day?

Franklin's Feelings (Social Studies)

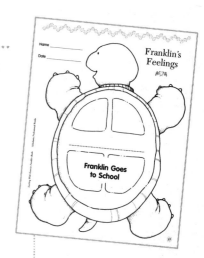

Make a feelings web to show the varied emotions Franklin felt on the first day of school. Copy and distribute the reproducible web on page 27. Work as a class or in small groups to complete the web by writing Franklin's name on the turtle shell and five of the emotions he felt on the arms, legs, and head. Invite children to complete the page in small groups. Then have each group share the emotions they wrote and tell when in the story Franklin experienced each feeling. Follow up by inviting children to talk about times they have felt the same emotions that Franklin experienced.

Calling Out Colors (Art)

Franklin told Mr. Owl that he knew all his colors. Turn to a colorful page in the book, such as the classroom scene which shows Franklin sitting alone at a table. Invite children to name all of the colors they see. Write the color names on sheets of construction paper cut in the shape of crayons, balloons, or other festive symbols. Post the shapes to make a word wall of colors in your classroom.

Make a Classroom Map (Geography)

Study the illustration that shows Franklin's friends playing at various learning centers in the classroom. Provide drawing paper and crayons. Have children work independently to draw a simple map that shows the layout of Franklin's classroom. They need not draw detailed items on the map; circles and simple sketches will do. Then have children work in small groups to draw a second set of maps, showing the layout of their own classroom.

Our Morning Routine (Social Studies)

What is the first thing Franklin did when he got out of bed? Reread part of the story to learn his morning routine—for example, waking up, packing his pencil case, waking his parents, eating breakfast, checking his book bag, and walking to the bus stop. Write each activity on its own sentence strip. As a class, put the strips in order on a pocket chart to make a simple time line. Then invite children to tell what they do in the morning. Write their activities on sentence strips. Put them in order to make a time line that represents the general morning routine: waking up, eating breakfast, washing face and hands, brushing teeth and hair, getting dressed, and so on. Most likely, your discussion will reveal slight differences: Some people dress before they eat, and others eat before they dress!

On Our Way (Social Studies)

Graph the ways children in your class travel to school. Photocopy the symbols below, and give one set to each child. (Create other symbols as necessary.) Let each child color and cut out the picture that depicts his or her usual way of getting to school. Have children use removable wall adhesive to attach their pictures to a graph that represents the various options.

Let's Look Ahead!
(Social Studies/Language Arts)

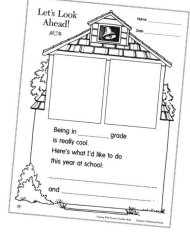

Make this banner during the first week of school to help children get to know one another and develop enthusiasm for the year ahead. Give each child a copy of the banner pattern on page 28. Inside the belfry, let children draw themselves doing two activities they would like to do this year in school. Ask them to complete the banner by writing their grade level, and two activities they would like to do. Hang banners side by side on a clothesline, at children's eye level but away from heavy traffic areas.

Pack and Go! (Critical Thinking)

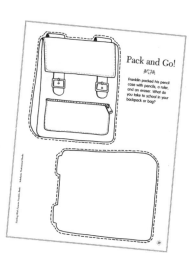

Give each child a copy of the backpack pattern on page 29. Have children cut out the pieces and staple them together to make a backpack. On a separate sheet of paper, ask children to draw four or five items they usually put in their backpacks or school bags. Have children color and cut out the items and drop them into their bags.

Language Hunt

Franklin had a busy first day at school! He made a building, sorted money, painted pictures, sat on the bus, bumped up and down, and hugged his mother. Help children find as many action words as they can in the story that tell what Franklin, his parents, his teacher, and his friends did throughout the day. Write each action word on an index card, and distribute the cards to volunteers. Have each volunteer read the action word and act it out for classmates to identify.

Book Links

Chrysanthemum
by Kevin Henkes
(Mulberry Books, 1996)

A young mouse thinks school is wonderful—until classmates make fun of her name.

Froggy Goes to School
by Jonathan London
(Viking, 1996)

Anxious over the first day of school, Froggy dreams about missing the bus and arriving at school in his underwear.

Meet the Barkers: Morgan & Moffat Go to School
by Tomie de Paola
(Putnam, 2001)

The Barker twins spend their first days of school finding friends and earning stars for class participation.

Vera's First Day of School
by Vera Rosenberry
(Holt, 1999)

Suddenly shy when arriving at school for the first time, young Vera distracts herself by watching a caterpillar, and ends up locked out of the building.

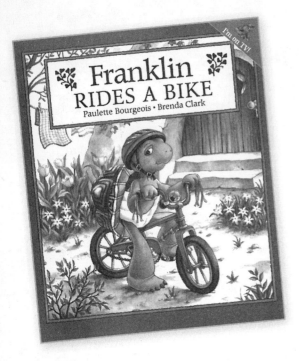

Franklin Rides a Bike

❧❧

(KIDS CAN PRESS, 1997)

Discouraged by his attempts to ride without training wheels, Franklin gives up bike riding, until he sees that he's missing out on fun times with friends.

The Story's Message

▲▲▲▲▲

⬡ Keep trying and you will succeed.

⬡ It takes practice to do something well.

Before You Read

Invite children to name important "firsts" in their lives, such as the first time they lost a tooth, learned to pump on a swing, or tied their shoes. Ask children to tell how they felt before and after accomplishing each milestone. Were they frightened or nervous beforehand? determined? excited? Were they relieved or happy afterward? proud? Open the book to the first page of the story, and show children the illustration of Franklin sitting on the steps. Ask them to predict what "first" the story will be about.

After You Read

 Talk about *Franklin Rides a Bike.* You might ask:

◎ How did Franklin feel when his friends could ride without training wheels and he couldn't? Why did he feel that way?

◎ In what way did Franklin think he was different from his friends?

◎ Riding a bike was difficult for Franklin. What activities were hard for his friends to learn? What did his friends do when they had difficulty?

◎ How did Franklin learn to ride his bike without training wheels?

◎ Have you ever had trouble learning something new? How did you feel? What did you do about it?

Follow up by inviting children to tell about times when they've felt left out or unhappy because they could not do something their friends could do. Discuss the importance of patience and persistence in learning new skills, and emphasize the value of encouragement that friends and family members can give at such a time.

Success Stories (Language Arts/Social Studies)

Have each child place a sheet of 8 1/2- by 11-inch white paper vertically on a flat surface. Have children fold the paper in half so the top edge meets the bottom. Then have them fold the paper again in the same way. As they unfold the page, the children will see four sections separated by fold lines. Have children number the sections in order, starting at the top, and draw arrows on the fold lines to represent a flow chart. (See illustration.) Next, invite children to think of an activity they've recently been successful with for the very first time, such as riding a bicycle, swimming, or jumping rope. Ask them to draw the activity on the flow chart, detailing four steps from the time they began to try the skill to the first time they did it successfully. Invite them to share their flow charts with the class as a guide in telling about the experience.

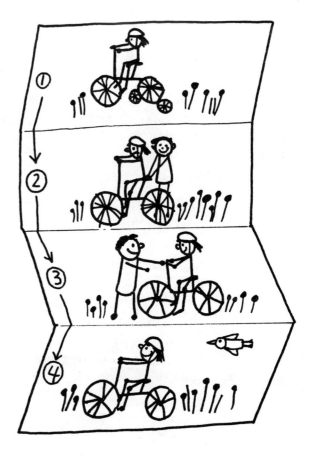

Franklin's Bike Helmet

by Paulette Bourgeois
(Kids Can Press, 2000)

Franklin wears his new helmet to a bike safety rally and almost gives it up when his friends poke fun.

D.W. Rides Again

by Marc Brown
(Little, Brown, 1993)

Practice and perseverance pay off when D.W. wants to leave training wheels behind and ride her own bike on two wheels.

Bicycle Safety: Safety Sense Series

by Nancy Loewen
(Child's World, 1996)

Two cartoon pups, Pickles and Roy, display safe and unsafe bike behaviors in this basic book on bike safety.

Shape Search (Math)

Shapes are everywhere, especially in illustrations as colorful and detailed as those in Franklin books. Reread *Franklin Rides a Bike* and invite children to study the illustrations and find as many shapes as they can. List the shapes they see, which might include circles (Franklin's bike tires), triangles (in the sandbox), and rectangles (on the tool box and in windows). Following the shape search, cut basic shapes from sponges and let children stamp them in paint or ink and then on paper. Have children use paint, markers, or crayons to turn the shapes into objects and scenery, such as a park swing, a wheel on Franklin's bike, and buildings.

What's the Scoop? (Language Arts)

In the story Franklin's friends enjoyed ice cream cones. Let children make their own ice cream cones to sequence story events. Cut out parts of a three-scoop ice cream cone for each child as follows:

◎ Cut one 4- by 2-inch brown triangle to serve as a cone.

◎ Cut three 3-inch diameter circles in pink, white, and light green to represent scoops of ice cream.

As a class, discuss the main events in *Franklin Rides a Bike* and list them on the chalkboard. Distribute the ice cream cone pieces. On the three scoops ask children to write and/or draw three scenes from the story. Have them glue the scoops together on their ice cream cones, with the top scoop showing the first event in the story, the middle scoop showing what happened next, and the bottom scoop showing what happened last. Have children use their cones as prompts to retell the story at school and at home.

Safety Riddles (Safety/Health/Language Arts)

Write the following riddles on sentence strips and place in a pocket chart one at a time. Read the riddles with children and have them fill in the missing words with words you have written or pictures you've drawn on small sentence strips. Then talk about the four safety rules described in the poem. For added challenge, cover the underlined words with blank strips of tagboard. Have children insert words for them or replace them with pictures to make a rebus.

Just like a <u>turtle</u>,
It has a hard <u>shell</u>.
A _____ would keep
Your <u>head</u> safe if you fell.

(helmet)

<u>Sidewalks</u> and <u>driveways</u>
Are safe spots to ride.
Stay away from the _____
When you play outside.

(street)

The <u>world</u> looks quite dark
When you ride at night.
Be sure your <u>bike</u> has
A <u>reflector</u> or _____ .

(light)

<u>Bikes</u> carry <u>people</u>
And are lots of fun.
How many should ride on your <u>bike</u>?
Only _____ !

(one)

Yes, I Can! (Social Studies)

Make turtle stories to show children's present and future achievements! Give each child a copy of page 30. Read the rhyme in each turtle. Have children write sentences in each turtle to tell about things they're proud of being able to do and things they're working on learning how to do.

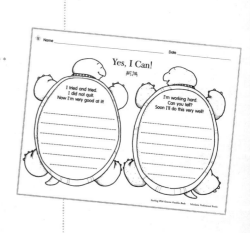

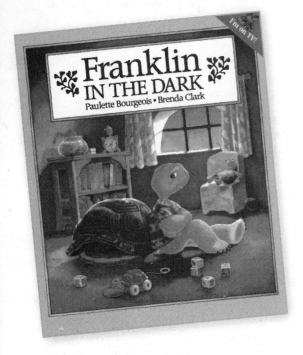

Franklin in the Dark

(KIDS CAN PRESS, 1986)

Fear of the dark keeps Franklin from crawling inside his shell. After talking to friends about their fears, Franklin finds a way to face his own.

The Story's Message

▲▲▲▲▲

- Everyone feels anxious or afraid sometimes.

- Every problem has a solution.

Before You Read

Display the cover illustration of *Franklin in the Dark*. Invite children to use picture clues to tell what time of day/night it is, how Franklin is feeling, and why they think he is sad or unhappy. Ask children what they think the story will be about.

After You Read

Ask questions to guide a discussion about the main points in the story:

- Why was Franklin afraid to go inside his shell?

- What animals did Franklin talk to about his fear of the dark?

- What did Franklin learn from talking with other animals?

- What did Franklin do to help himself sleep in his shell again?

- What helps you feel better when you feel afraid of the dark?

Take Action (Drama)

Talk about the idea that Franklin didn't just complain about his problem; he found a way to solve it. Divide the class into small groups. Give each group an index card with a common fear written on it, such as fear of certain animals, darkness, deep water, loud noises, heights, being alone, visiting doctors, and receiving vaccinations. Have each group act out the fear for the class and invite classmates to suggest ways to handle it.

Turtle in the Shell (Language Arts)

Make an interactive bulletin board display to reinforce word families:

◉ Cut 6 turtle shells and 36 turtle heads from colored tagboard.

◉ Label each shell with a specific word family, such as -at, -op, or -ed. Label each group of 6 heads with letters that complete the word family, such as c, h, m, p, s, and b for the -at family. Laminate all shells and heads.

◉ Cut a slit on the left side of each shell so that a turtle head can slip easily into it. Staple the shells in a row on a bulletin board, being careful not to staple the slits.

◉ Place the turtle heads in an envelope or tagboard "pocket" stapled to the bulletin board.

During free time, let children slide turtle heads into shells to make words. As they work, they'll soon discover that many different words can be formed from the same word family shell!

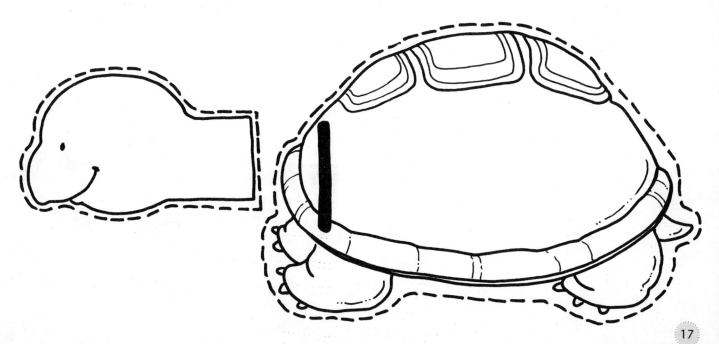

Brave Martha

by Margot Apple
(Houghton Mifflin, 1999)

Each night, Martha trusts
her cat, Sophie, to keep
watch for monsters under
her bed. When Martha
can't find Sophie one
night, she must check for
monsters on her own.

The Monster in Harry's Backyard

by Karen Gray Ruelle
(Holiday House, 1999)

Nighttime noises sound like
bears when Harry camps
out in his backyard for the
very first time.

Facing Fears (Critical Thinking)

Franklin used a night-light to help
himself feel comfortable in his dark
shell. How else might Franklin have
handled his fear of the dark? Help
children rewrite the story so that
Franklin, or any other animal in the
story, finds a different way to deal
with his/her fear, such as sleeping with a stuffed animal or
listening to music before falling asleep. First, help children organize their
thoughts and information by using the chart on page 31. In the second
column (beside each animal), have children write or draw what the animal
fears. In the third column, have children draw what the animal does to
conquer the fear. In the last column, ask children to draw what they would
do or have done themselves.

I'm Afraid (Drama)

Assign one volunteer to act as Franklin, saying, "I'm afraid of small, dark
places and I can't crawl inside my shell. Can you help me?" Invite volunteers
to pose as the duck, lion, bird, polar bear, and as Franklin's mother. Have
them respond to Franklin's request with words from the story or with
examples of other fears and their solutions. Invite additional volunteers to
pose as animals not mentioned, telling what they might fear and how they
handle their fears. For example, a monkey might be afraid of high places.
How can it get bananas and swing from trees?

Three or More (Language Arts)

In many stories for young readers, characters repeat phrases or actions three
or more times as the story progresses. This repetition strengthens skills in
language development, comprehension, and prediction. In *Franklin in the
Dark*, Franklin continually says, "I'm afraid of small, dark places and I can't
crawl inside my shell. Can you help me?" Invite children to think of other
picture books that employ this kind of repetition, such as *The Little Red
Hen, Chicken Little, A Mother for Choco*, and *Are You My Mother*? Encourage
children to bring in picture books that show repetition, and share them with
the class throughout the week.

Language Hunt

Stage a word hunt through the pages of *Franklin in the Dark*. Challenge children to find adjectives, or words that describe, such as *small*, *dark*, *creepy*, *slippery*, and *deep*. Write each word as a heading on a turtle shell or balloon cut from colored paper. Beneath each word, have children list items or animals it describes—for example, for the word *creepy*, children might list *ghosts*, *skeletons*, and *spiders*. For a challenge, you might invite children to combine adjectives—for example, *small and dark* (*Franklin's shell, a broom closet,* and *a fireplace*).

What's Under the Shell? (Math)

Add and subtract in the shelter of shells. Divide the class into pairs. Give each pair a walnut (turtle) shell and 10 unpopped popcorn kernels. Have one partner hide some kernels under the shell, leaving the rest beside it. The other partner must count the kernels beside the shell and determine how many are underneath, based on the total number of kernels. Both partners must then write a number sentence describing what they see. For example, if they start out with 10 kernels and only four are showing, the number sentence would be $4 + 6 = 10$ or $10 - 4 = 6$.

Franklin's Bad Day

❧❧❧

(KIDS CAN PRESS, 1996)

Saddened by the fact that his good friend moved away, Franklin wakes up in a grumpy mood. Nothing seems to go right for him all day, until he shares his feelings and finds a way to help himself feel better.

The Story's Message

▲▲▲▲▲

⬡ Sometimes it helps to talk things out with others.

⬡ Doing kind deeds can help us feel good.

Before You Read

Share the cover of *Franklin's Bad Day*. Ask children to tell how Franklin is feeling and to explain how they can tell he is grumpy. Encourage them to use picture clues to determine the season in which the story takes place.

After You Read

Draw the outline of a turtle on chart paper. Draw a grumpy face on the turtle. Inside its shell, write the many ways Franklin's body language told others he was feeling grumpy: he frowned, crossed his arms, slammed a door, stomped his feet, and so on. Then talk about the story and the reasons why Franklin was grumpy. Some questions you might ask include:

◎ When did Franklin first start feeling grouchy?

◎ When did you first discover the reason Franklin felt grumpy?

◎ Why was Franklin so upset about kicking over the block castle?

◎ How did Franklin feel after he talked with his father about missing Otter? Why do you think he felt that way?

◎ How do you think Franklin felt after he wrote to Otter? Why did he feel that way?

◎ Have you ever felt angry or upset and talked with someone about it? How did you feel after you talked it out? Why?

What Went Wrong? (Language Arts)

Have each child fold an 8 1/2- by 11-inch sheet of paper into four sections. Ask children to draw a picture in each section that shows something that went wrong on Franklin's bad day. For example, they might depict the following story events: a friend moving away, a broken cup, a missing puzzle piece, and a tumbled block castle. Help children write captions for each picture. Compile the drawings to make a class book of Franklin's difficulties on that day.

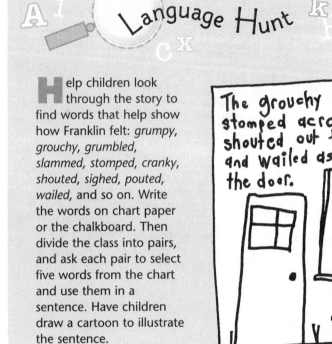

Language Hunt

Help children look through the story to find words that help show how Franklin felt: *grumpy, grouchy, grumbled, slammed, stomped, cranky, shouted, sighed, pouted, wailed*, and so on. Write the words on chart paper or the chalkboard. Then divide the class into pairs, and ask each pair to select five words from the chart and use them in a sentence. Have children draw a cartoon to illustrate the sentence.

The grouchy giant stomped across the floor, shouted out the window and wailed as he slammed the door.

Ahh!

Block Brigade (Math)

Franklin knocked over a block castle that he and Otter had built. Divide the class into pairs. Provide each pair with two identical sets of 10 blocks and have partners try to build identical block towers, or have them work together to build one castle. Then have each pair count the blocks and group them in different ways to determine how many of each kind they have: how many rectangles, how many squares, how many red blocks, how many blue, and so on. If time permits, pool group information together and make a collaborative graph.

Book Links

Glenna's Seeds
by Nancy Edwards
(Child & Family Press, 2001)

A young girl slips marigold seeds into her neighbor's flowerpot, setting off a chain of kindness that blooms around the neighborhood.

Grumpy Bunnies
by Willy Welch
(Charlesbridge, 2000)

Three grumpy bunnies rise but don't shine as they start getting ready for school. By the time they reach the playground, however, they begin to get into the day.

I Like Your Buttons!
by Sarah Lamstein
(Albert Whitman, 1999)

A young girl's compliment to her teacher sets off a string of kind behaviors.

Mr. Tanen's Ties
by Maryann Cocca-Leffler
(Albert Whitman, 1999)

When a school principal is told to stop wearing his outlandish, cheerful ties, he becomes discouraged and cannot come to school.

Tip

▲▲▲▲▲

Warm-Blooded Hibernators

bats
chipmunks
ground squirrels
hamsters
hedgehogs

Cold-Blooded Hibernators

frogs
toads
lizards
snakes
turtles

Fact or Fiction? (Science)

Franklin's Bad Day takes place in the winter. Are real turtles active in winter? In real life, no. Turtles, like other reptiles, cannot remain active when the weather grows cold. Instead, they hibernate, keeping their bodies warm enough to stay alive. Freshwater turtles burrow into the muddy bottoms of ponds and streams to hibernate. Land turtles, such as Franklin, bury themselves in soil or under vegetation left over from harvest. Share this knowledge, and use it as a springboard to a study of animals that hibernate. (See Tip, left.) Hand out copies of page 32 and have children color and cut out the animals on the dotted lines, leaving the chart intact. Have students identify each animal and discuss whether it is warm-blooded (a mammal) or cold-blooded (a reptile or amphibian). To help them decide, discuss additional characteristics shared by mammals (feed young on mother's milk) or by reptiles and amphibians (most hatch from eggs). Then have children glue the animals in the appropriate column of the chart.

Reach Out to Others
(Social Studies)

Franklin turned his day around by making a scrapbook for Otter. Invite children to tell of times when they have felt better because they did something nice for someone else even though they were feeling unhappy. (Enlarge and copy the badge shown here.) Make one badge for each child in your class. Have children read the sentence "I helped someone else!" and draw on the badge a picture of themselves doing a kind deed for someone else on a day when they might not have been feeling up to it.

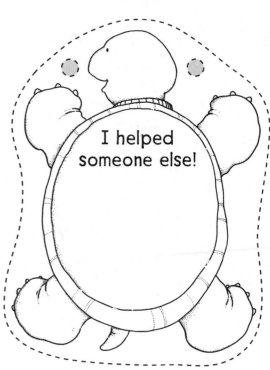

I helped someone else!

Sequence the Story Events (Language Arts)

Give each child a copy of page 33. Have children cut out the sentences at the bottom and glue them in order on the mini-book pages. Invite them to draw pictures to go with each sentence. Then have them cut apart the pages and staple to make a book. Encourage children to use the book to retell the story to classmates and take it home to share with their families.

Franklin Fibs

(KIDS CAN PRESS, 1991)

Franklin tells a lie to impress his friends. He soon tells other lies to keep that one going, and eventually learns that telling the truth is best.

Before You Read

Ask children to tell you the meaning of the word fib. Explain that a fib is a lie; it is something untrue. Ask children to give reasons why people might fib. Ask: Is it a good idea to tell a fib? Why do you think that?

After You Read

Talk about the main idea of the story. You might ask questions such as:

◎ Why did Franklin fib in the first place?

◎ Did Franklin's friends believe he could really eat 76 flies in the blink of an eye? Why not?

◎ What parts of the story showed you that they didn't believe him?

◎ What did Franklin do to earn his friends' trust again?

Invite children to think about times in their lives when they have been tempted to tell a lie instead of the truth. Ask them to tell why they were tempted to lie. Talk about possible consequences of lying. Help children understand that even very small lies break down trust. People will be less likely to believe or depend on a person who lies than they would a person who tells the truth.

The Story's Message

⬡ It is important to always tell the truth.

⬡ Honesty will earn the trust of others.

Franklin said,
"I can swallow
seventy-six flies
in the blink
of an eye."

↓

Franklin pretended
to have a sore throat.

↓

Franklin's friends
laughed at him.

↓

Franklin couldn't
eat or sleep.

↓

Franklin admitted
he had lied.

↓

Franklin baked and
ate a whole fly pie.
He learned not to lie.

Truth or Consequences (Social Studies, Language Arts)

Help children make a flow chart of cause and effect in the story by tracking the first fib Franklin told and its consequences, emphasizing the idea that honesty is best. Use sheets of colored construction paper (8 1/2- by 11-inches) to make the chart. Invite children to describe the first lie Franklin told. Write it on the first sheet of paper. Then write the consequences that followed on separate sheets. Post the pages in order on a wall or bulletin board, with arrows between them to represent a flow chart.

Fly Pie Math (Math)

Franklin loves Fly Pie! Use the Fly Pie pattern on page 34 to strengthen math skills. You might use it in one of the following ways:

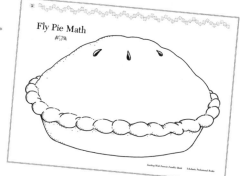

Fly Pie Math

◎ Give children several copies of the reproducible pattern. Have them cut out the fly pies and staple them together to make a shape book. Have children glue raisin "flies" on each page to make a counting book that goes from 1 to 5 or from 1 to 10.

◎ Make one copy of the reproducible for each child. Have children cut out the pie and glue on a handful of raisins to represent flies. Line up the pies on a table in the classroom. Let children estimate the number of flies on each pie, writing each estimate on a slip of paper and dropping it into a cup in front of the pie. Count the flies. How many on each pie? How many in all?

Exaggeration Station (Language Arts)

Franklin could eat lots of flies, but not 76 in the blink of an eye, as he professed. Explain the meaning of exaggeration, and invite children to brainstorm things people say that sound like exaggeration, such as, "She put a ton of peas on my plate," or "I have one hundred things to do." Provide paper and have children draw themselves doing something they can do—but to an exaggerated extent.

Pond Pop-Ups (Science)

Ask each child to choose one animal or insect from a pond scene in the story. Have children go home after school and find two facts about their animal or insect. Have them write the facts on a sheet of paper and bring them back to school. At school, demonstrate how to make a pop-up picture. (See below.) Have children make a pop-up of their animal or insect and write the two facts along the bottom of the page. Have children share their pop-ups with the class and also display them in the classroom for children to look at and earn from during free time.

To make a pop-up:

1. Fold a sheet of 8 1/2- by 11-inch paper in half.

2. Cut two equal, parallel slits (about 2 inches each), beginning at the fold.

3. Unfold the paper. Push the cut area through, as shown. Fold the paper again and crease all fold lines well.

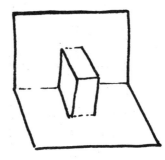

4. Unfold the page. This time, the cut-out area should pop up to form a ledge.

5. Draw a picture of the animal or insect being studied. Cut out the drawing and glue it to the area that pops up when the paper is unfolded.

Peek Into the Pond (Science)

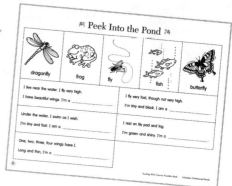

Ask children to study the pond scenes in *Franklin Fibs* and identify the many different insects and other forms of life found there: flies, dragonflies, beetles, snails, fish, butterflies, lizards, caterpillars, frogs, and so on. Let them use watercolors to create a pond scene. Give each child a copy of page 35. Have children cut out the riddles and glue them to the bottom of their pictures. Ask them to color and cut out the animals, and glue them in the appropriate places. Invite children to read each riddle, find the matching animal, and write in the animal's name.

The word *fibbed* means the same as *lied*. Help children find other examples of words in the story that share the same meaning, such as *boasted*, *bragged*, and *crowed*. Then challenge them to be on the lookout throughout the school day for words that share the same meaning, such as *talk* and *chat*. Whenever a child makes a connection, have him or her write the two words on a slip of paper and drop it in a box near your desk. At the end of each day or week, read the entries in the box. Draw one at random and give the contributor a small favor or privilege in reward.

Name _____

Date _____

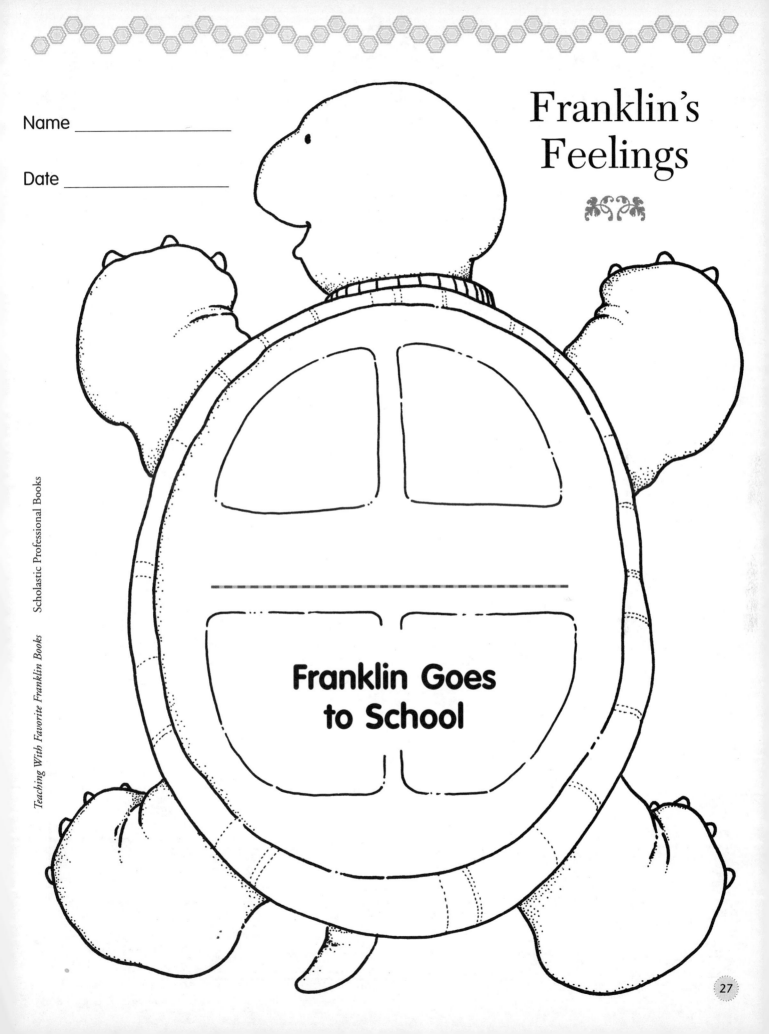

Franklin Goes
to School

Let's Look Ahead!

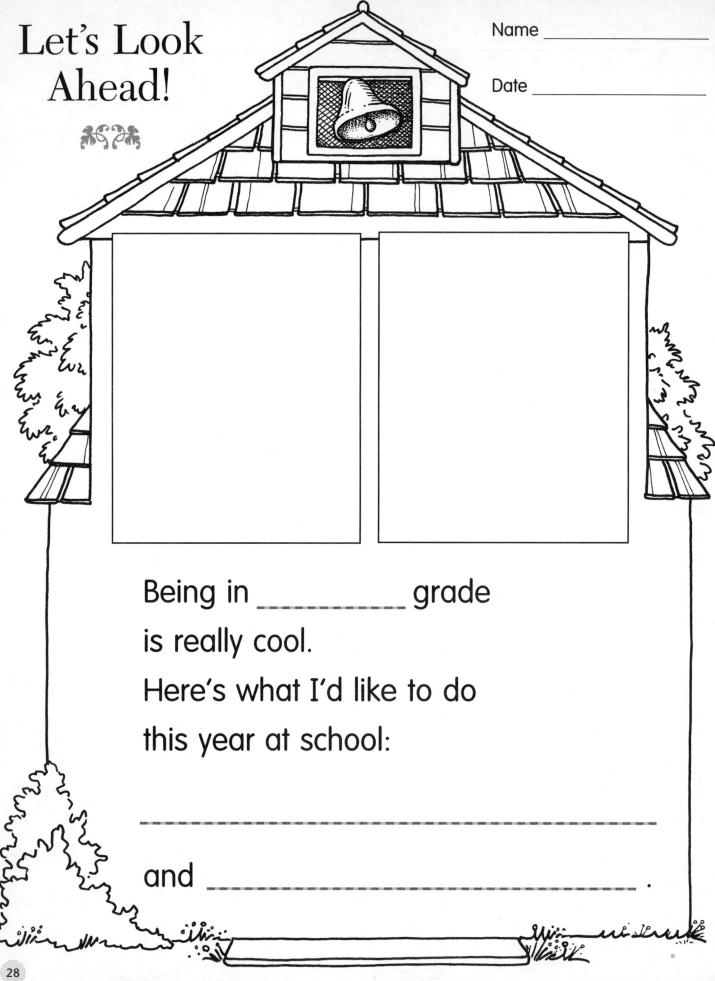

Name _____

Date _____

Being in _____ grade
is really cool.

Here's what I'd like to do
this year at school:

_____

and _____ .

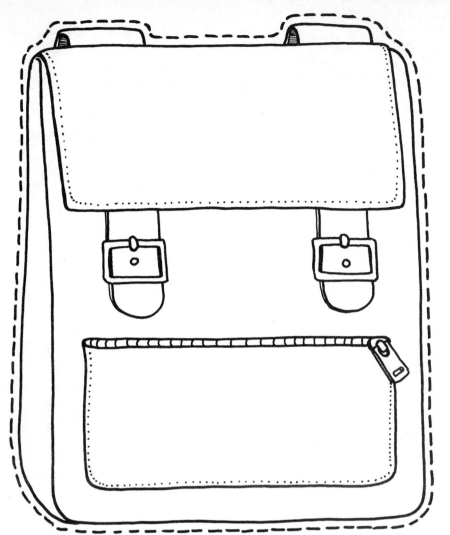

Pack and Go!

Franklin packed his pencil case with pencils, a ruler, and an eraser. What do you take to school in your backpack or bag?

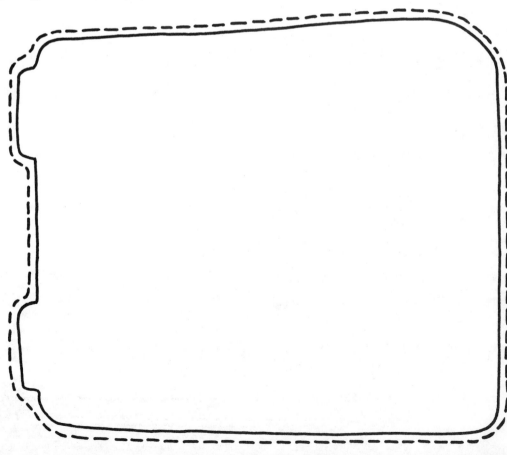

Name _____

Date _____

Yes, I Can!

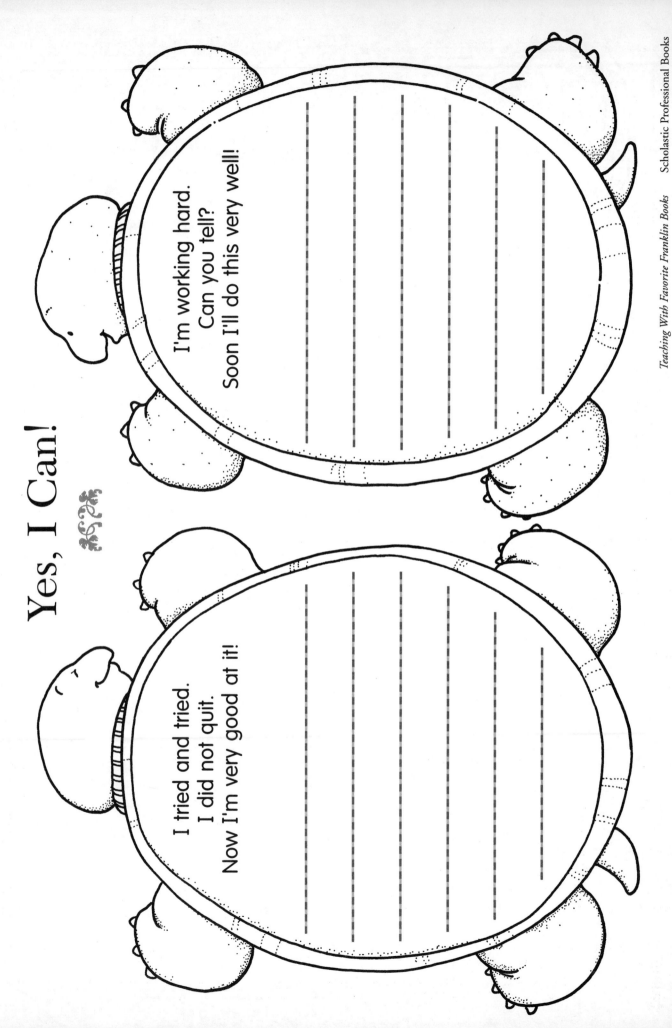

I tried and tried.
I did not quit.
Now I'm very good at it!

I'm working hard.
Can you tell?
Soon I'll do this very well!

Teaching With Favorite Franklin Books   Scholastic Professional Books

Name _____

Date _____

❧ Facing Fears ❧

Animal's Name	What the Animal Fears	What the Animal Does	What I Would Do

❧ Fact or Fiction ❧

Warm-Blooded Hibernators	Cold-Blooded Hibernators

✂

hamster	frog	lizard	ground squirrel	snake

turtle	chipmunk	bat	hedgehog	toad

Teaching With Favorite Franklin Books   Scholastic Professional Books

❧ Sequence the Story Events ❧

[_____]
①

[_____]
②

[_____]
③

[_____]
④

Franklin kicked over his block castle.	Franklin woke up in a grumpy mood.
Franklin made a scrapbook for Otter.	Franklin and Bear went sledding.

Fly Pie Math

❀❧

Teaching With Favorite Franklin Books   Scholastic Professional Books

✿ Peek Into the Pond ✿

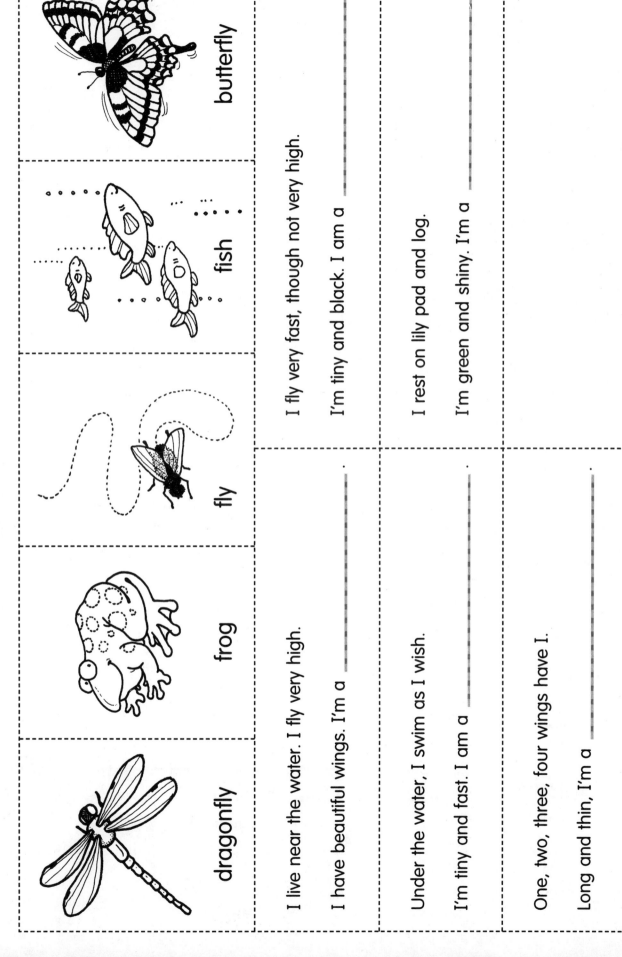

butterfly

fish

fly

frog

dragonfly

I fly very fast, though not very high.

I'm tiny and black. I am a _____.

I rest on lily pad and log.

I'm green and shiny. I'm a _____.

I live near the water. I fly very high.

I have beautiful wings. I'm a _____.

Under the water, I swim as I wish.

I'm tiny and fast. I am a _____.

One, two, three, four wings have I.

Long and thin, I'm a _____.

Teaching With Favorite Franklin Books   Scholastic Professional Books

Franklin Is Bossy

❧❦❧

(KIDS CAN PRESS, 1993)

Franklin clashes with his friends when he tries to tell them what to do.

The Story's Message

▲▲▲▲▲

⬡ It is important to treat others with kindness and respect.

⬡ People don't want to play with those who are bossy.

Before You Read

Invite children to tell what it means to be bossy. Ask them whether they think being bossy is a good thing and why they feel that way. Then hold up the cover of *Franklin Is Bossy* and read the title aloud. Invite children to predict what they think the story will be about. Write their predictions on chart paper, and compare them to the actual story line once you have read it aloud.

After You Read

Use these questions to guide a discussion about *Franklin Is Bossy*:

◎ Why didn't Franklin's friends want to play with him?

◎ What specific things did Franklin do that his friends did not like?

◎ Why didn't Franklin listen when Bear told him he wasn't being fair?

◎ When did Franklin realize he had to change his behavior?

◎ What might Franklin do to teach himself to be fair instead of bossy?

Conflict and Resolution (Social Studies)

Have children identify conflicts that arose in the book and consider the ways the characters handled them. To do this, write the following sentences on tagboard strips. Place them in a pocket chart individually, as you discuss each one.

◎ "I don't want to play with you anymore!" shouted Bear.

◎ "No way!" shouted Bear. "I don't want to play with you. You are too bossy."

◎ Franklin played alone for another whole day.

◎ Franklin insisted on being pitcher again.

Regarding each conflict, you might want to ask: What is the conflict? How did Franklin respond? Do you think Franklin and his friend(s) handled the conflict the right way? Why do you think that? What else might they have done?

Friendship Fits! (Social Studies/Art)

As a class, brainstorm to make a list of things friends can do to get along, such as:

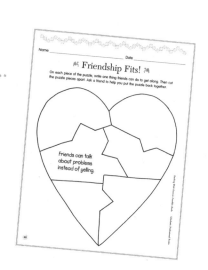

◎ Friends can share.

◎ Friends can talk about their feelings.

◎ Friends can speak calmly instead of yelling.

◎ Friends can tell each other what they want to happen.

◎ Friends can apologize when they are wrong.

◎ Friends can take turns.

Give each child a copy of page 48. Invite children to choose five statements from the list, or come up with additional things friends can do to get along, and write them on the puzzle pieces. Have children cut the puzzle pieces apart carefully. Then divide the class into pairs and have each pair work together to assemble both puzzles.

Book Links

Hooway for Wodney Wat
by Helen Lester
(Houghton Mifflin, 1999)

Despite an impediment that has taxed his self-esteem, Rodney Rat stands up to a class bully.

Horace and Morris But Mostly Dolores
by James Howe
(Atheneum, 1999)

Three young mice learn that belonging to exclusive clubs often happens at the expense of satisfying friendships.

Little Miss Bossy
by Roger Hargreaves
(Price Stern Sloan, 1998)

Little Miss Bossy is just that—bossy—until Wilfred the Wizard casts a spell that changes her outlook.

Act Out the Story

(Drama)

Franklin Is Bossy offers plenty of lively conversation, making it a prime candidate for a classroom play. Invite volunteers to take on the parts of Franklin, Bear, Duck, Goose, Fox, Beaver, Rabbit, Franklin's father, and Mole. (Children can read lines directly from the story or make up their own.) Involve additional volunteers in drawing scenery and finding props such as chairs, baseball bats, and a bag of marbles. Perform the play for other classes in your school.

How Does It Feel? (Language Arts)

Let children take the point of view of Franklin's friends, drawing a cartoon (with a bubble caption) that tells how they felt when Franklin wanted to choose all the games and be the star player.

Calling All Voters! (Social Studies)

Emphasize the benefits of voting over having one person make all the decisions for a group. Ask children what would happen if only one child in the class was allowed to decide what the whole class could do during free time. Most likely, children would prefer to have a say in how they spend such precious time. That's where voting comes in handy. Make a graph entitled, "What Shall We Do During Free Time Today?" Ask for suggestions, and list these down the left column of the chart. Invite each child to cast a vote by placing a sticker on the graph beside the activity they prefer. Tally the votes, and choose the top two as the free-time activities for the day. Change the graph topic often for extra voting opportunities!

Franklin's Secret Club

(KIDS CAN PRESS, 1998)

Franklin starts a secret club, and some of his friends feel left out. When his friends start a club of their own, Franklin finds a way to bring them all together.

Before You Read

Ask children to name any clubs or organizations to which they belong—for example, Drama Club, Cub Scouts, Brownies, or local sports teams. Then ask whether children have ever formed clubs of their own. Invite children to talk about what might be involved in having a club of one's own—finding a place to meet, planning special club activities or membership cards, and so on. Then show the cover of *Franklin's Secret Club*. Read the title aloud. Ask children to use picture clues to determine what the story might be about and who apparently is (and is not) a member of Franklin's secret club.

After You Read

Discuss the main ideas of the story. You might ask questions such as:

◎ Why did Franklin decide to have a secret club?

◎ Why did Franklin limit the number of friends who could be in his club?

◎ How do you think Fox, Beaver, and Raccoon felt when they found out Franklin had a club and they couldn't belong to it?

◎ When did Franklin realize how it felt to be left out?

◎ What did Franklin do to bring the friends together again?

The Story's Message

▲▲▲▲▲

⬡ Being considerate of other's feelings helps keep feelings from being hurt.

⬡ Finding fun things to do is a way to bring friends together.

Book Links

Horace and Morris But Mostly Dolores
by James Howe
(Atheneum, 1999)

Three friends discover that a club made for everyone is the best club of all.

The Cool, Crazy Crickets to the Rescue
by David Elliott
(Candlewick Press, 2001)

Members of a neighborhood club raise money to help save a cat.

Annie Bananie Moves to Barry Avenue
by Leah Komaiko
(Delacorte Press, 1996)

When Annie Bananie moves in, life in the neighborhood gets exciting.

Macaroni Math (Math)

Make macaroni bracelets as Franklin did in his secret club, using colored ziti and string or fabric-covered elastic. Reinforce patterning by asking children to create patterns as they make their bracelets, placing macaroni in repeating order by color, size, or shape.

Clubhouse in a Box (Social Studies)

Let children create their own miniature clubhouses out of shoeboxes and art supplies such as construction paper, glue, glitter, felt scraps, fabric scraps, ribbon, lace, wallpaper, yarn, empty spools of thread, cubes of wood, and markers or paints. (You may want to have children draw a map to determine the layout of their clubhouses first.) Invite children to name their clubs and suggest activities club members might do together. Encourage global thinking by having children design clubs that serve the needs of others, such as by raising money to help the homeless, to beautify the community, or to brighten the day for residents of senior citizen homes.

Compare the Clubs (Language Arts)

The Secret Club and the Adventure Club offered fun and excitement to their club members. How were the two clubs alike? In what ways were they different? Have children study the pictures and reread the story to find clues. Make a simple chart to compare and contrast the two clubs.

The Secret Club	The Adventure Club
Met in a small hideaway	Met in a campsite
Ate muffins	Dug for dinosaurs
Made tin-can telephones	Planned trip to the moon
Made macaroni bracelets	Made boats to float
Had club handshake and password	Had club handshake and password
Had a treasure hunt	Went swimming
Wrote invisible letters	Swung on a tire swing

Join the Color Club (Language Arts)

These poetry mini-books teach words for colors. Give children copies of the mini-book on page 49. Have children cut out the pages, put them in order, add a construction-paper cover, and staple to bind. Read the poem together, then have children color pictures on each page that match the color described. Try these activities to learn more with the mini-book:

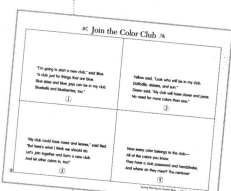

◉ Have children use blue crayon to underline the words in the poem that name items that are blue: blue skies, bluebells, blue jays, and blueberries. Have them use yellow, green, and red crayons to underline words that name items of those colors.

◉ Write the first three verses of the poem on tagboard strips and place in a pocket chart. Underline the words that name items that are blue, yellow, green, and red. Have children replace those items with others of the same color. For example, instead of *clover* and *peas*, children might suggest *inchworms* and *grass*.

What's the Password? (Language Arts)

Franklin's club members thought up their own special club password (Fizzle-Fazzle, Diddle-Daddle, Ding-Dong-Blueberry-Bop!) and handshake (flapped arms, wiggled fingers, wrinkled noses, slapped hands twice, and tickled once). Let children work together to create a password for their classroom, as well as a special class greeting. Write it on chart paper. Review the password and class greeting daily until children know it by heart.

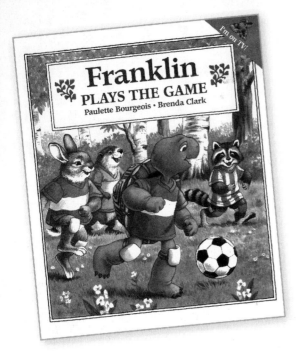

Franklin Plays the Game

❧❧❧

(KIDS CAN PRESS, 1995)

Franklin and his soccer teammates learn to work together and have fun while they build new skills.

The Story's Message

▲▲▲▲▲

⬡ Teams do their best when everyone works together.

Before You Read

Show children the cover of *Franklin Plays the Game.* Invite them to tell what sport Franklin and his friends are playing. Then make a quick graph of the sports children in your classroom play. Starting with soccer, ask children to raise their hands if they belong to a soccer team. Record that number of children on the graph. Then find out how many children participate in other popular sports and physical activities, such as baseball, softball, dance, and gymnastics. Write these on the graph as well. Then talk about the results. How many sports are played in all? Which sport is played by the most children? the least?

After You Read

Talk about the main points in *Franklin Plays the Game.* You might ask:

◎ Why were Franklin and his teammates discouraged?

◎ What advice did Franklin's coach give his players?

◎ How did Franklin and his teammates discover a way they could play well together? What did they do about it?

◎ What did Franklin and his friends learn about teamwork?

◎ What does the word "teamwork" mean to you?

Teamwork Training (Physical Fitness)

Play games that build fitness and encourage teamwork. Examples include playing soccer, throwing bean bags into buckets, and running relay races that involve a Franklin theme: the turtle crawl, the rabbit hop, and so on. You might also try a team game with an academic theme: Tic-Tac-Toe Math. Here's how:

◉ Place a solid color shower curtain on the floor. Turn the curtain into a tic-tac-toe play mat by drawing on it a grid with nine squares.

◉ Divide the class into teams. Ask each team to stand in a line, single file.

◉ Read each group a math fact in turn, and let the person at the head of the line answer it. If the answer is correct, that team member gets to throw a beanbag onto the grid. If the answer is not correct, the other team gets a turn. Players move to the back of the line after answering, whether or not their answers are correct. The first team to place three beanbags in a row wins.

Marshmallow Manners (Social Studies)

Teamwork relies on cooperation. Children who know how to cooperate can work together effectively in the classroom as well as on the sports field. Use the following activity to reinforce skills in cooperation:

◉ Divide the class into groups of four or five. Give each group a cupful of mini-marshmallows and at least 30 toothpicks.

◉ Invite children to work together to create a structure, using only the materials provided. Stress that all group members must help decide what structure the group will make and how it will be constructed.

◉ When each group has finished, combine several groups and have them work together, connecting their structures to form one large structure. Then work as a class, connecting all of the structures to make an enormous one that will not topple over!

Book Links

The Little Red Hen (Makes a Pizza)
by Philemon Sturges
(Dutton, 1999)

Little Red Hen shops alone for the ingredients and labors without help to create a large pizza. When she invites friends to share the meal, they respond by offering to wash the dirty dishes.

D.W. Flips
by Marc Brown
(Little, Brown, 1987)

Try, try again is the theme here as D.W. strives to master a gymnastic flip.

Allie's Basketball Dream
by Barbara E. Barber
(Lee & Low, 1998)

When Allie takes her new basketball to the park and tries to play ball with the boys, they tell her the sport isn't meant for girls. Undaunted, Allie practices until she can shoot as well as anyone.

Language Hunt

Looking for a fun way to divide the class into groups? Keep a supply of word family fruit on hand. To make the fruit, cut from colored construction paper five each of lemons, apples, oranges, grapes, and bananas. Select a piece of fruit at random and write on it a word that belongs to a word family, such as *map* from the *-ap* family. On the four remaining kinds of fruit, write four additional words from the family (*sap, lap, tap,* and *cap,* for example). Do not limit the word family to one type of fruit; use all five kinds. Then choose another word family, and write its words on five different pieces of fruit. Continue until you have four or five word family groups. Mix up the fruit and put it in a small bowl. When it's time to divide into groups, have children pick a piece of fruit from the bowl at random and link up with other children who hold fruit from the same word family.

Soccer Sums (Math)

This fast-paced game reinforces counting, addition, and subtraction skills. Give each child a copy of page 50. Have children cut out each soccer ball. Divide the class into pairs. Have each partner place his or her soccer balls facedown in a stack. At the same time, both partners flip over the top ball in their stack. The player with the highest number of dots wins both soccer balls. The first player to collect all of the soccer balls from his or her partner wins the game. Other ways to play include:

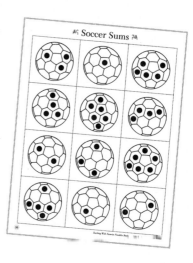

◎ Partners add the number of dots on both soccer balls. The first player to say the correct sum wins both soccer balls.

◎ Partners subtract the lower number of dots from the higher. The first player to say the correct answer wins both soccer balls.

◎ Partners add to find the sum of dots on both soccer balls and write a number sentence to show how they reached that sum (for example, 1 dot + 3 dots = 4 dots). Partners then write number sentences to show other ways to reach the same sum.

Franklin Has a Sleepover

(KIDS CAN PRESS, 1996)

Excitement fills the air as Franklin prepares for his very first sleepover.

Before You Read

Show children the cover of *Franklin Has a Sleepover*. Ask them to predict what they think the story is about. Children will probably guess that Bear is going to stay overnight at Franklin's house. Encourage them to predict what the sleepover might entail: What kinds of games might Franklin and Bear play? Where might they sleep? What special foods might they eat?

After You Read

Guide a discussion about *Franklin Has a Sleepover* with the following questions:

◎ How did Bear feel when Franklin asked him to sleep over? How could you tell?

◎ What did Franklin do to get ready for the sleepover?

◎ What special items did Bear pack that told you he was getting ready for a sleepover and not just a regular visit?

◎ Have you ever slept over at a friend's house or a relative's house? What did you do there that made it extra special?

Invite children to tell about times when they've slept over at a friend's or relative's home and felt scared or unhappy at bedtime. Talk about reasons why people sometimes feel that way and what they can do to feel better.

The Story's Message

▲▲▲▲▲

⬡ Even new events can go smoothly when you take the time to prepare yourself.

45

Book Links

Ira Sleeps Over

by Bernard Waber
(Houghton Mifflin, 1973)

When Ira's invited to his first sleepover, he wonders whether he should bring his cherished stuffed bear.

Pajama Party

by Joan Holub
(Grossett & Dunlap, 1998)

Girls share pizza, stories, and pillow fights at an overnight party young readers will enjoy.

Rabbit's Pajama Party

by Stuart J. Murphy
(HarperTrophy, 1999)

Rabbit invites his friends to a sleepover party—and readers must sequence the story.

Porcupine's Pajama Party

by Terry Webb Harshman
(HarperTrophy, 1990)

Porcupine invites Otter and Owl to spend the night, but who will watch out for the monsters?

Fly Pie, Please! (Science)

Help children compare the foods that Franklin and Bear ate with real foods they eat. Let them browse the illustrations in *Franklin Has a Sleepover* and make a list of the foods (and drinks) they see, including grapes, bananas, apples, oranges, carrots, sandwiches, coffee, pie, honey, marshmallows, hot dogs, blueberry muffins, oatmeal with bugs, and juice. Most of these are foods and drinks that are part of a healthy human diet as well. Briefly discuss the importance of eating healthful foods. Then challenge children to add to the list other foods that a turtle and bear might find tasty, such as raisin bread, bread with flies instead of raisins, and honey-coated cereal.

Blueberry Math (Math)

Franklin loves foods with bugs or berries inside. With this in mind, make mini-muffins and purposely drop eight to ten blueberries, raisins, or chocolate chips into each one before baking. Give each child a muffin, and cut the muffin in half. Have children count the berries, raisins, or chips they see on each half of the muffin, add the two to determine how many in all, and write a number sentence to describe what they see. Before the children eat the muffins, divide the class into groups of four. Let group members look at (without touching) each other's muffins and count the number of berries/raisins/chips in all, the number of muffins in the group, the number of muffin halves, and so on. At the end of the lesson, let children eat the muffins for a tasty approach to subtraction! (Check for food allergies first.)

Help Bear Pack (Language Arts)

Give children a copy of the patterns on page 51, and have them cut out the pictures of things Bear might pack to bring to Franklin's sleepover. Ask children to sort the pictures in any or all of the following ways:

◎ by initial consonants (*pants, pillow, popcorn*)

◎ by type of item (*clothing the friends might wear, foods they might eat, toys they might enjoy, things that might help them sleep*)

◎ by number of items shown (*three balls, three berries, three books*)

You might also wish to have the children glue the pictures on a strip of paper so that the picture names are in alphabetical order: *balls, berries, books, candy,* and so on.

Language Hunt

Have children hunt through *Franklin Has a Sleepover* to find words that they associate with fun times, such as *campfire, hot dogs, marshmallows, flashlight, toys,* and *sleepover*. Encourage them to find these words in all parts of the story from beginning to end. Draw a huge toy box on craft paper, and cut a 6-inch slit where the box would normally open. Staple the box to a bulletin board, being sure to secure it on all sides so that paper inserted will not slip out. Give each child six index cards. As they find words in the story, have children write them on index cards and slide them through the slot and into the toy box. After everyone has had a chance to find and deposit six words, "open" the toy box and take out the words. Hold them up for the class to read aloud. Then staple them to the outside of the toy box for display throughout the week.

The Perfect Sleepover (Language Arts)

Invite children to draw their own pictures and write several sentences telling what they would like to do at a sleepover at their home or someone else's. What would they like to eat? What games or activities would they most enjoy? Would they rather sleep in a sleeping bag or bed? a tent or a bedroom? outside or inside? What would make the sleepover an exciting and memorable event?

Name _____ Date _____

❧ Friendship Fits! ❧

On each piece of the puzzle, write one thing friends can do to get along. Then cut the puzzle pieces apart. Ask a friend to help you put the puzzle back together.

Friends can talk about problems instead of yelling.

Teaching With Favorite Franklin Books   Scholastic Professional Books

🍀 Join the Color Club 🍀

"I'm going to start a new club," said Blue.

"A club just for things that are blue.

Blue skies and blue jays can be in my club.

Bluebells and blueberries, too."

①

Yellow said, "Look who will be in my club:

Daffodils, daisies, and sun."

Green said, "My club will have clover and peas.

No need for more colors than one."

②

"My club could have roses and leaves," said Red.

"But here's what I think we should do:

Let's join together and form a new club

And let other colors in, too!"

③

Now every color belongs to the club—

All of the colors you know.

They have a club password and handshake,

And where do they meet? The rainbow!

④

Soccer Sums

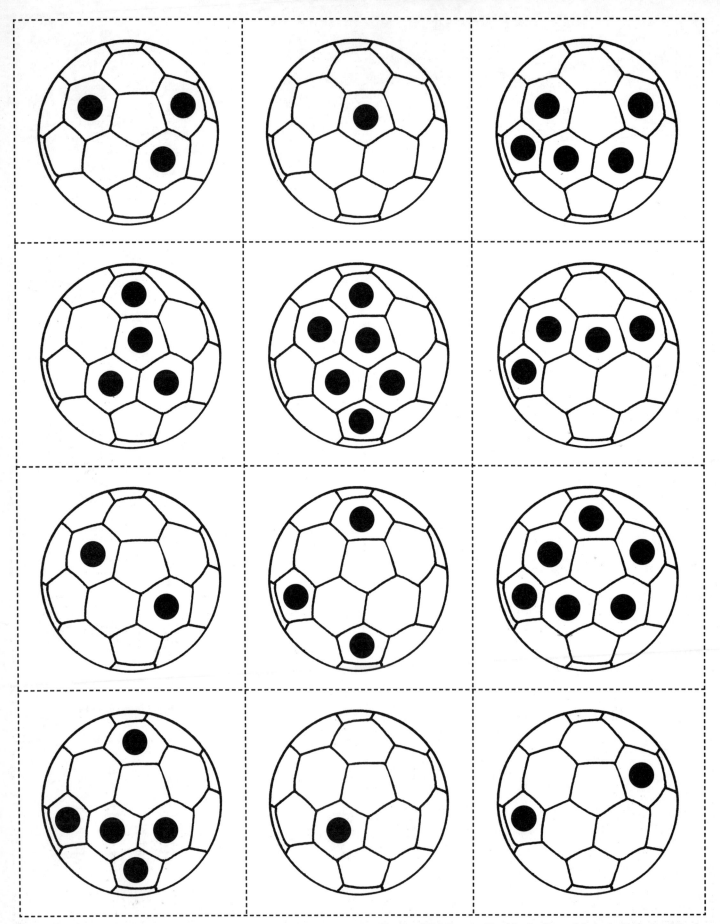

Teaching With Favorite Franklin Books   Scholastic Professional Books

Help Bear Pack

balls	toothpaste	popcorn
cars	berries	books
pajamas	puzzles	cookies
pillow	slippers	toothbrush
socks	candy	pants

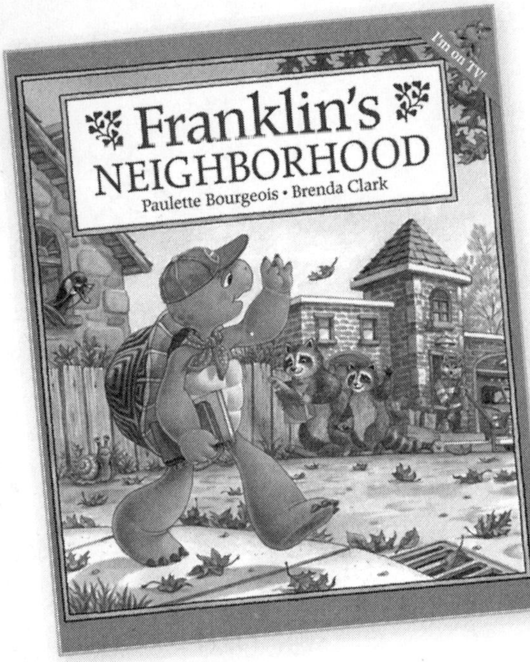

Franklin's Neighborhood

(KIDS CAN PRESS, 1999)

Franklin travels around his neighborhood to see what he likes best.

The Story's Message

- People are an important part of what makes a good neighborhood.

Before You Read

Ask children to define the word *neighborhood.* Help them recognize that a neighborhood is a community in which people live, work, and play. Invite children to think about the neighborhood in which they live. Then show the cover illustration on *Franklin's Neighborhood.* Invite them to tell what they see.

After You Read

Discussion Starters

Talk about the story. You might ask questions such as:

- Why did Franklin have a hard time choosing the best thing about his neighborhood?
- What did Franklin do to help himself figure out what he liked best?
- What neighborhood places did Franklin's friends like best?
- What did Franklin think about each time someone mentioned a place in the neighborhood?
- How did that help Franklin decide what he liked best?

Invite children to close their eyes and think about their neighborhood. When they open their eyes, hand out drawing paper and crayons. Ask them to draw what they like best about their neighborhood, whether it be a place or a person.

My Neighborhood Game
(Social Studies)

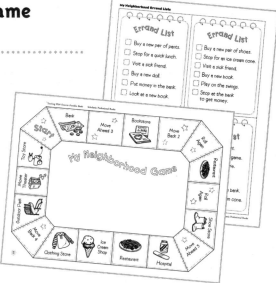

Play a board game with a personal touch! Give each child a game board. (See page 61.) Have children personalize their game boards by drawing pictures of stores, restaurants, and outdoor areas in their city or town. Divide the class into small groups and give each group one copy of page 62, which provides errand lists for up to four players. Have each group use only one player's game board and one die at a time, plus one errand list per player. To play the game, children place plastic milk caps or other markers on START and roll the die to see who goes first. In turn, players roll the die and move around the board. Each time a player lands on a location named on his or her errand list, the player makes a check mark beside it. The first player to land on and check every location on his or her list wins the game. (Children can go around the game board as many times as necessary to complete their list.) Have players swap lists for subsequent games.

Make a People Chain (Art)

Help children make a paper chain of four people, connected at the hands. On each person, have children draw the face and features of a person they value in their neighborhood. To make the chain:

◎ Cut a sheet of 8 1/2- by 11-inch paper in half lengthwise.

◎ Hold the paper strip horizontally. Fold it in half from left to right.

◎ Fold it in half again.

◎ Draw a figure on the paper. Be sure the ends of both arms and both legs touch the fold line. Open to reveal four connected persons.

Book Links

Night on Neighborhood Street
by Eloise Greenfield
(Puffin, 1996)

Life on a city street is brought to light in this series of poems about neighborhood life.

Dr. Friedman Helps Animals
by Alice K. Flanagan
(Children's Press, 2000)

Vibrant photographs detail a day in the life of a veterinarian. Part of the Our Neighborhood Series.

Raising Cows on the Koebel's Farm
by Alice K. Flanagan
(Children's Press, 1999)

Readers take a photographic journey to a neighborhood farm. Part of the Our Neighborhood Series.

What Zeesie Saw on Delancey Street
by Marjorie Priceman
(Aladdin Picture Books, 2000)

Seven-year-old Zeesie attends an ethnic celebration with her parents, learning much about her Jewish heritage.

Who Are the People in My Neighborhood?

(Social Studies/Language Arts)

The riddles below describe people children might expect to see in a neighborhood or community. Write the riddles on sentence strips, and place them in a pocket chart for children to solve. Then let children replace the underlined words to make their own riddles about workers they know, such as school employees, bus drivers, and other familiar faces in their community.

Look <u>in the post office</u>.
You will find me.
I <u>sort letters and packages</u>.
Who might I be?
(postal worker)

Look <u>in the fire station</u>.
You will find me.
I <u>help put out fires</u>.
Who might I be?
(fire fighter)

Look <u>in the library</u>.
You will find me.
I <u>take care of books</u>.
Who might I be?
(librarian)

Make Franklin Character Cards (Language Arts)

Give children six unlined index cards each. Ask them to choose six characters from any Franklin book they've read so far. Have children draw a picture of each character on one side of an index card. On the back of the card, ask them to write the character's name and facts about the character, such as his or her age, teacher, closest friends, favorite foods, hobbies, interests, and so on. Allow time for children to read and enjoy each other's cards.

Ask children to look through the story and find the names of places in a neighborhood, such as stores, a hospital, and the berry patch. Make a list of all the places named in the story, and then have children circle those that are found in their own neighborhood or community. Invite children to add to the list, naming places not mentioned that are found in their own community. Ask each child to choose a place from the list and draw a picture of it on a sheet of plain paper. Tape or staple the pages together, end to end, and display in the classroom as a community banner.

Franklin and the Thunderstorm

(KIDS CAN PRESS, 1997)

Franklin is frightened during a thunderstorm, and his friends help cheer him up.

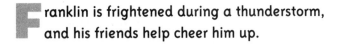

Before You Read

Show children the cover of *Franklin and the Thunderstorm*. Ask them to tell what is happening in the picture and how Franklin seems to be feeling. Invite them to tell how they feel when they see and hear a thunderstorm. Why do they feel that way? What do they do when a thunderstorm comes near?

After You Read

Ask these questions to help children think about the story:

◎ How did Franklin feel when he knew a storm was coming? What parts of the story tell you that? Why did Franklin feel that way?

◎ Did Fox make the right choice by staying outside? Why do you think that?

◎ Why didn't Fox's mother think the tree fort was a safe place to stay in a storm?

◎ What did Franklin do when he heard thunder? Why did he do that?

◎ How do you feel when a thunderstorm starts? What do you do?

The Story's Message

▲▲▲▲▲

⬡ A thunderstorm is a weather condition with thunder, lightning, and sometimes rain.

⬡ Following basic safety rules can help keep you safe during a thunderstorm.

Storms

by Seymour Simon
(Mulberry Books, 1992)

The author explains
thunderstorms, hurricanes,
and tornadoes with concise
text and vivid photographs.

**Weather: Poems for
All Seasons**

by Lee Bennett Hopkins
(HarperTrophy, 1995)

This delightful collection
of poems describes various
weather conditions with
just the right blend of
rhyme, silliness, and
word play.

Language Hunt

Ask children to find words and phrases in the story that have something to do with weather: *thermometer, barometer, sky, clouds, rain, wind, blow,* and so on. Make a large cloud out of white craft paper. Write the weather words on the cloud. Post it on the wall under the heading "Our Weather Words." Throughout the week, invite children to write sentences and stories that use weather words.

Know Nature Signs (Science)

Invite children to recall details from the story that told Franklin and his friends a storm was about to hit: the wind became stronger, rain began to fall, dark clouds filled the sky, the animals' fur felt funny because of the cooler air blowing in, the animals smelled extra moisture in the air. Ask them to share other signs of impending weather conditions, such as the sky filling with a thick, white blanket of clouds before snowfall, and leaves blowing backward before a rainstorm. For the next several weeks, invite children to pause at times throughout the school day, check weather conditions outside, and make weather predictions for the day.

From Bolt to Clap (Math)

Scientists say that every five seconds that elapse between a bolt of lightning and a thunderclap indicates that the thunderstorm is one mile away. Let children use this information to create math problems such as this for their classmates: Jenny counted 10 seconds between lightning and thunder. How far away is the thunderstorm?

Thunder Tales (Language Arts)

Hawk blamed the noises of thunder on cloud giants playing drums in the sky. Snail said it came from giants bowling. Talk about reasons why people make up silly stories about thunder and lightning (most often to overcome fear). Then challenge children to think up their own fictitious causes for thunder and lightning. Have each child write a sentence or two that describes what they think is causing the noise and the light and illustrate their explanations. Staple their pages together to make a class book entitled "What's Going on in the Sky?"

Make a Shell Shape Book (Science)

Franklin pulled himself into his shell for protection when he was scared. Talk about how most species of turtles are able to pull their head, legs, and tail into their shell for protection. Cut out and staple together five identical turtle shapes to make a shape book for each child. (You can use the pattern on page 30.) Have children write and illustrate one fact about turtles on each page of their book. They might include these facts for starters:

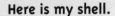 Turtles are the only reptiles with a shell.

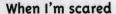 Turtles are cold-blooded.

◎ Most turtles can pull their head, legs, and tail into their shell.

Share a Franklin Fingerplay (Language Arts)

Read the poem aloud and demonstrate the finger movements once. Then invite children to recite the poem with you several times, imitating your motions.

I am a turtle.	(Stretch out two fingers of right hand. Hold others under.)	
Here is my shell.	(Hold out left hand, cupped.)	
It's strong and hard. It fits me well.	(Cover right hand, fingers exposed, with cupped left hand.)	
When I'm scared	(Shake fingers slightly as if trembling.)	
And want to hide, I simply pull Myself inside!	(Draw fingers under to hide beneath cupped hand.)	

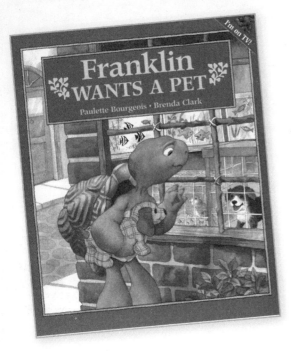

Franklin
Wants a Pet

(KIDS CAN PRESS, 1994)

Franklin's parents say he can have a pet, and Franklin must choose just the right one for himself.

The Story's Message

▲▲▲▲▲

- ⬡ Different pets need different kinds of care.

- ⬡ People choose pets for different reasons.

Before You Read

Hold up the cover illustration of *Franklin Wants a Pet*. Ask children to tell what is happening in the picture. What kind of store is Franklin looking into? What does a pet store sell? Have children identify the animals they see in the picture. Then have them look at the animal Franklin is holding. Ask children whether the animal is real, and how they are able to tell. Invite them to predict what the story will be about.

After You Read

Discussion Starters

Talk about the main ideas in *Franklin Wants a Pet*. You might ask:

- ◎ Why did Franklin want a pet?
- ◎ What did Franklin's parents need to know before they could allow Franklin to have a pet?
- ◎ Was Franklin ready to have a pet? What parts of the story told you this?
- ◎ Why did Franklin choose a fish for a pet instead of a puppy or another animal?
- ◎ If you had been Franklin in the story, which pet would you have chosen? Why?

Make a Pet Cube (Language Arts)

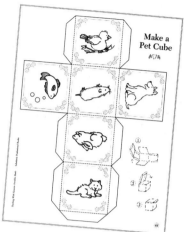

Give each child a copy of the pet cube on
page 63. Help children cut out and assemble
their cubes, then invite them to identify the
six animals pictured—all animals Franklin
considered having as a pet. Divide the class
into pairs and use the cube in any of the
following ways:

◎ Have partners take turns rolling the
cube. When they see which animal lands on
top, they can recall details from the story and tell why Franklin felt the
animal was or was not the right pet for him.

◎ Have both partners roll their cubes at the same time and try to roll
matching animals.

◎ Let groups of six or eight children roll their cubes at the same time.
After each roll, stop and count how many of each kind of animal landed
on top. Graph the results, or have children write number sentences
about them: 3 dogs + 3 fish = 6 animals.

◎ Have partners roll the cubes and take turns telling what steps are
involved in caring for the pet whose picture lands on top, for example,
feeding, exercising, and grooming needs.

Best Pet? You Bet! (Social Studies)

What's the most popular pet? Let your class be the judge. As a class,
brainstorm pets people might own. With a show of hands, have children
narrow the list to the top six animals. Then have children cast their vote for
their favorite of the six. Record the results on several different kinds of
graphs to demonstrate how various graphs can be used to show the same
information. Along with the traditional picture graph, you might try
making a bar graph or pie chart, or label six canning jars and have children
drop a marble in the one labeled with their pet of choice.

Meet My Pet (Language Arts)

Invite children to write about a pet they have at home or a pet they would
like to have. Encourage them to describe their pet: its color, size, shape,
features, how it feels to the touch, what it does, and what they like most
about it. Encourage children to bring in or draw pictures of their pet and
share them with the class.

Book Links

Harry the Dirty Dog
by Gene Zion
(HarperTrophy, 1976)

When Harry runs away to
avoid a bath, he gets so
dirty that his coat changes
color. Back at home, Harry
must find a way to wash
his coat so his owners will
recognize him again.

Hamsters
by Kate Petty
(Barron's Juveniles, 1993)

What's it like to care for a
hamster? Readers will learn
what it takes in this
photographic tribute to a
tiny household pet. Part of
the First Pets Series.

Who Am I? (Critical Thinking)

Cut out the shapes of familiar pets (bird, cat, bunny, puppy, frog, hamster, fish, guinea pig, gerbil, turtle, horse, snake, and so on) from workbooks, nature magazines, and coloring books. Tape one picture to each child's back. Allow children to walk around the room and ask questions to determine which animal he or she is wearing: Is it furry? Does it have wings? Does it live in water? Once they discover the answer, children should sit down, but still answer the questions of those around them.

That's Good! That's Bad! (Language Arts)

Imitate the style of the classic "that's good/that's bad" mode of storytelling with a good/bad chart. On posterboard, make a three-column chart. Down the left column, write the names of the six animals Franklin considered having as a pet. For each name, invite volunteers to tell one thing that might be good about having such a pet and one thing that might be bad about it. Write these in the two columns beside each animal name, under the headings "What's Good" and "What's Bad."

What's in a Name? (Language Arts)

FISH. What does it spell? Have children write an acrostic using the letters of an animal's name. For example, an acrostic for fish might be:

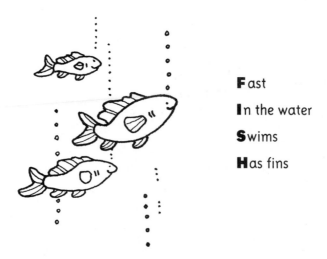

Fast

In the water

Swims

Has fins

Have children write their acrostics on construction paper cut in the shape of the animal.

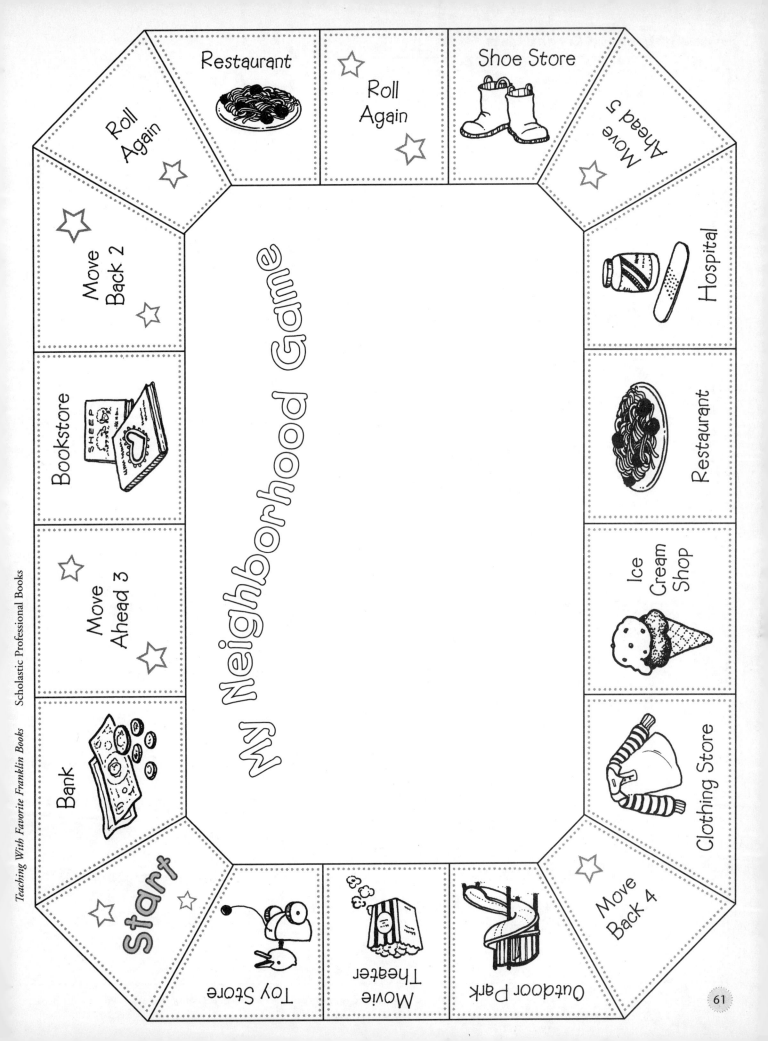

My Neighborhood Game

Restaurant

Roll Again

Shoe Store

Move Ahead 5

Roll Again

Move Back 2

Hospital

Bookstore

Restaurant

Move Ahead 3

Ice Cream Shop

Bank

Clothing Store

Start

Toy Store

Movie Theater

Outdoor Park

Move Back 4

Errand List

- ☐ Buy a new pair of pants.
- ☐ Stop for a quick lunch.
- ☐ Visit a sick friend.
- ☐ Buy a new doll.
- ☐ Put money in the bank.
- ☐ Look at a new book.

Errand List

- ☐ Buy a new pair of shoes.
- ☐ Stop for an ice cream cone.
- ☐ Visit a sick friend.
- ☐ Buy a new book.
- ☐ Play on the swings.
- ☐ Stop at the bank to get money.

Errand List

- ☐ Buy a new pair of sneakers.
- ☐ Buy a new shirt.
- ☐ Look at a new book.
- ☐ Sit down in the park.
- ☐ Watch a new movie.
- ☐ Buy a stuffed dog.

Errand List

- ☐ Stop for breakfast.
- ☐ Buy a new board game.
- ☐ Watch a new movie.
- ☐ Buy a new book for a friend.
- ☐ Put money in the bank.
- ☐ Share an ice cream cone.

Teaching With Favorite Franklin Books   Scholastic Professional Books

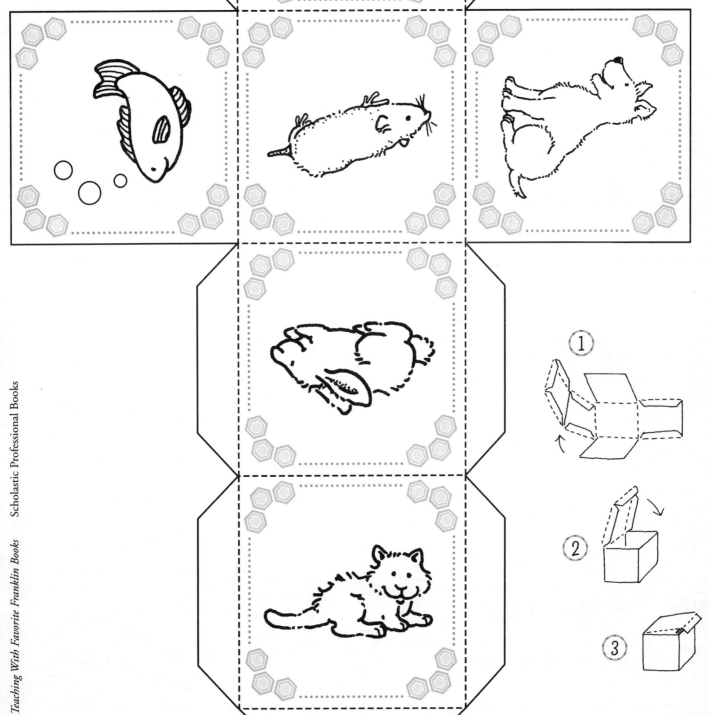

Make a Pet Cube

A Franklin Festival

Wrap up your study of Franklin with a classroom celebration.
Plan to include some or all of the events listed here on this special day.

Bake Fly Cookies

Prepare homemade Franklin Fly Cookies—oatmeal cookies with raisins—that children will love to eat! (You'll find tasty recipes on oatmeal canisters.) If possible, let children help measure and place dough on cookie sheets for baking.

Freeze Bug Pops

Franklin would enjoy frozen juice pops with bugs inside. To make them, pour orange juice or fruit punch into 3-ounce paper cups. Make one for each child in your class. When the pops are slightly frozen, drop gummy worms cut into small pieces (to represent bugs) into the juice and stand a craft stick in each cup. When the pops are completely frozen, let children peel away the paper cups and enjoy!

Make Story Sacks

Write various events from the Franklin stories on slips of paper and place in a shoebox or small bowl. Place 12 paper lunch bags on the floor, each labeled with the title of a Franklin story you've studied. One at a time, have children pick a strip, read the event out loud, and drop it into the bag labeled with the story it came from. For example, the slip that reads "'I'll never score a goal,' said Franklin sadly." belongs in the bag labeled *Franklin Plays the Game.* Continue until all of the slips are sorted.

And the Winner Is...

Which is the most popular Franklin story among your classroom voters? Take a poll and find out. Display Franklin books on a chalkboard ledge or tabletop, with a paper lunch bag beneath each one. Have children write their name on a slip of paper and drop it in the bag beneath the Franklin story they liked best. Have children tally and record votes on a graph, and then analyze the results.
   You might ask:

◎ Which Franklin story received the most votes?

◎ Which Franklin story received the least votes?

◎ How many people voted for the top Franklin book?

◎ Which stories, if any, received the same number of votes?

◎ What are the top five Franklin stories, according to the children in our class?

Tip

▲▲▲▲▲

Check for food allergies before serving cookies and juice pops.